POEMS BY

JAMES WHITEHEAD

domains

LOUISIANA STATE UNIVERSITY PRESS

Some of these poems have appeared in *Motive,
Discourse, Evidence, New Campus Writing,* and
LRU Forum, to which grateful acknowledgment
is made.

FOR GEN

CONTENTS

domains

Floaters

Dallas Tanksley would run up on our yard
As skinny and fairly goodnatured as ever to say
His Daddy had spotted a floater, come and see . . .

Floaters were drowned people, turgid, not hard,
Surfacing around the bend about twice a year,
And usually a Negro from St. Louis
Bringing a stern sight down to all of us
In the country where only the deaths of the aged were clear.

My father said they jumped from the Barracks Bridge,
Being poor and debtors to boot and deeply in love
With something he never explained just then. Like a glove
Full of mother's cold dishwater, or maybe fudge
Left out a week and getting whitish from sugar
Crystals, they were pulled onto our sand bar.

Two Voices

Taggart says he gives them what they want—
They come to him in the night blind drunk and broke,
And he sews them up free, without a shot.
With his coarse thread he has the art to raise
Great scars from ear to ear, and he does just that—
It's part of a ritual they've done for years.
"I send them proud to the fields and gins," he says.
"With their heads pulled back that way, those bucks are grand,"
He says. "They brag after all we did it raw."

Thompson says you can hear their cries to the creek,
And he nearly objects, believing the fish in their way
Are offended—or at least that so much yelling
Can make a cat hook-shy, and anyhow
It's always Saturday night and Sunday morning
After the tonk fights and when he fishes.
"And not only that," Thompson says, "it's giving
Sorry dreams to my children." And almost angry:
"You'd think a doctor and all, he'd think of his neighbors."

Delta Farmer in a Wet Summer

Last summer was hot and dry, a better time—
Two cuttings at the dock and two knocked up
In the fields, and a crop to fill the wagons full.
There were prime steaks and politics at night,
Gin to nine and bourbon after that—
By God, we raised some handsome bales and hell,
Then went to New Orleans as usual.

But now it rains too long, too little sun
To stop the rot. Rain beats down on the roof
At night and gives sad dreams—black bolls—
And the Thunderbird will have to go. You can smell
It on the evenings, like the smell of a filthy
Bed, or wasted borrowed money, the stink
Of a bloated dog when finally the water's down.

. . . in California they say it's dry.
They irrigate consistently, don't count
The weather in when going to the bank,
And that's damned smart, except they've got no woods
Or sloughs to crowd the fields, and dogs get killed
But rarely drown—and I think our bitch, stretched hide
And stench, contains the element of
    chance a Christian needs.

One for the Road

Night full and the click of the lighter after love
   is almost kind, and careless, too, like the laugh
   I leave with the sullen bills. And that's the way
   it is, if not the way it ought to be,
   down this Memphis road . . .

I ought not pay, I know,
   but your way of going is easier than most—
   and even now, after I pull first drag,
   you're not half bad, and next to the rig you're the best
   of love I've got. You're a little soft in the pooch—
   but hell, I'm not a Natchez cock myself . . .

And it's not your legs or hair, God knows, not those,
   not easy things to get your mind around—
   it's your way of washing after all's got done,
   and something like fun among the common sounds—
   nails split, teeth gapped, who gives a damn . . .

And then the soft of loss with the coming sun,
   when you sleep me off like a dream almost of sin.

Common

More often than not my wife holds common sway
Over common things—and yet not commonly—
Like my fancy aunt flung *common* to my dismay
Against a friend of mine one day.

"He,
That Tanksley boy down by the river, is *common*—
All of them are common, every last Tanksley
There ever was." And that meant Dallas Tanksley
And Dallas Tanksley's solid mother who ran
For sheriff once to try and get good done.

My wife has yet to seek a public office—
And her children have never gone hungry—but I'm sure
She would, if she felt she should—if any face
In our house showed common need, or plain despair.

A Local Man Goes to the Killing Ground

They formed the ritual circle
   of Chevy trucks. Tracks were there,
   worn tires, the still prints in the mud
   and thin grass. My light could barely suggest
   the glare that fell on the men they killed.

It was an intimate thing—
   all of them drawn in so close
   they didn't bother with guns
   or the normal uses of the knife.
   It was done with boots.

I walked around that quiet place
   and tried to reclaim the energy
   that must of course remain in the earth.
   It keeps the truth to itself
   as they will, when they stride out of court.

By then it was all grey, false dawn—
   and I thought it was like stomping
   a fetus in the womb, a little
   skin between the killers, the killed,
   for the dead were curled in their passive way.

The Flood Viewed by the Tourist from Iowa

They paddled the street as fast as rowboats can,
To fetch back to the Parlor the Negro dead:
Embarrassment . . . that made no sense. A flood—
It was a flood, seven inches of rain
Through a single span of day and night, and all
In trouble just about the same. But still,
When word of the bodies came, the Public Will
Was wonderfully active. It was like Plague Call.

I suppose there was something ancient in it,
Men fearing the dead will walk, or maybe swim . . .

You should have seen those white men hurry to it . . .
None of the Negroes seemed nearly so grim
About it. In fact, one black, with a strange wit,
He sang a Freedom Song, hanging from a limb.

For Flannery O'Connor

Hell, you know we have to see some god
In the weeds, and a little botched with all that sun.
Like the town drunk or idiot or killer
He keeps on coming for dinner like a friend
We can't re*member where he knew our brother* . . . ?
Gobbles the chicken. Says, "I'm the one—
I'm the one Billy done in, and you—
You got to pay like you was him."   Billy!

Christ, we hadn't seen that fool for years—
Him with his teeth and all his crazy fears
If he stayed at home he couldn't have his fun . . .
Your freak stays on the place until he's through
With us. Insults. Rapes the women. Breaks
The mower. Weeds. Weeds. Weeds. Shouting—
"That sunnavabitch Billy, he's the one . . .
And I'm doing it all for *your* sakes . . . for your sakes!"

The Opinion of an Interesting Old Man

It's plain damned hard to lose yourself these days . . .
or at least you can't the clean way you once could . . .
gone for a week without boiled water and food,
then turning up in town misunderstood

with the whole place mad because they'd planned to say
nice things when sure you wouldn't come their way
again. It's a crying shame the way they're rude
enough to hunt you down within a single day

and just before you get that taste of fear
and just before you feel you're about to pray.
You hear them thrashing through the brush, when you're nude
with love of being lost. They think you're crude

if you plead you'd like to stay. They always intrude
like parents who are appalled by curious play,
and they trade with the oldest lie: "It's for your good,
dear friend. We've come to help you out," they say.

And out you go. Be sure they knew you would.
Be sure they'd rather have you alive than dead.

The Young Deputy

It was Leroy Smith we meant to find
   in the slough, the old river, with hooks
   but didn't. It was two others, or halves
   of two, the big man's torso, the small
   man's thighs, which made the sheriff sick
   in the boat. It wasn't one man no matter
   how hard he tried . . .

Eaten by fish was one answer.
   Maybe gar. Drowned, with rope
   still strung from the thick wrist, and a little
   chain around the bottom's ankle.

   (considering conflicting reports
   of disappearance from various places
   they might have been a dozen men)

Then it got to be a joke about
   the burial: one grave or two,
   since they'd got fixed as a single thing
   in everybody's mind. Smith,
   he never came to light, and it seemed
   to figure that the one good grave
   could somehow cover all three—and more,
   said a few with furious souls.

There'd be, I thought, if things were right,
  a fine day of picnicking,
  preaching to a big mixed audience,
  and in the nearest pine one buzzard,
  glossy, hunkering, with a confused gaze.

McComb City, August, 1958

This town is silent. No wind
All day would cross the balustrade
And now in the streets the night
Dogs are gay and on parade,
Mad with an old moon.

I hear them begin to whine their thin curses
Against all signs of rain.
I watch them pad toward dawn where rage is.

After Hours

. . . of course of course there are those fat mother-lovers
who shoot guns and talk all hours (me sometimes)—
and the ones who make it a way of life watch out
for them. Noisy boys who never liked
their decent brothers and never liked hard work
much better—their monkeyshines, their wrecked Fords
and dirty women make them think they're big men.

But look at them at peace in honest houses now,
where the serious wrecks are with words—a busted participle
the compound fracture, the wife's bleeding heart
from his curse like a knife.

They claim three dead on the road—one girl—and really
crow their griefs in the raw hours, their past
and sin the staple of talk, as grease and bread
is their regular food, their tripe . . .

. . . so they hunt like marines in season and buy seatbelts—
so they dream of the bitch who wet the grass with blood
back then, remembering all, like their war or their one
best game—so they stare like cocks down a line
drawn on the chicken yard—show welts a buddy gave.
I'd say it's right to call them men.

And one more thing before I go—but quieter:
we all had better go easy on the lately reformed.
Everything in anyone that comes to grips with anything
has something to be said for it.
I know you've noticed my ring.

Taking a Break

Taking a break to smoke
We rested on a ridge
And Wyatt finally said
That in these woods were ghosts,
Slave dead and bad
Classicists who gave
Them Greek and Roman names.

He'd seen some stones the year
Before: *Plato, faithful*
Slave of Royal Green;
Marcus . . . such as that.
He said this stand was their dream
And far more civilized
Before we came to count trees.

He told how spirits stay
Because of violence
Done on the man's body,
How they stay confused
Around their old place
Until someone explains
Their killer has died too.

Our Picayunes made wraiths,
And it wasn't his way to joke—
But he wasn't afraid: "Ghosts—
But I'm not afraid. No more
Than snakes." And we didn't fear snakes.
They were common, and
We had our boots and razor

Blades—heavy khakis.
You can always bleed
Against a snake, and it seemed,
Hearing Wyatt talking
Flatly of ghosts around,
That something similar
Would certainly do for them.

The Wreck

One night just out of the woods
I came on a wreck, or what seemed
To be a wreck—the car
In the field was upside down,
The wheels still turning around,
And in the car, piled upside
Down, was the smiling driver
Whose body still seemed sound.

He opened his old Ford door
And crawled straight through the weeds
To where I nervously stood—
"Get up (if you can)," I said.
And he did. "I got my pride,"
He said: "Christ, how she ride!"
He grinned and tested his legs:
"She stays over there," he said,

"And I better, by God, start walking,"
And pointed toward a shed
Not far away, where the light
Was burning . . . his wheels still turning . . .

Desertions

Among books and tools some miles
From town, he gardens a little and speaks
Of her return:

My spirit describes the genuine
Concern a dear friend holds, as one
Might hold a tender bulb for planting.
Hers was a rout of sense, the sort
A child commits on pilfered wine,
An antic attitude for which
A plot of time must be set out
That growth become secure . . .

His trowel cuts a cup of mulch
To fix in the smallest window box:

Decay is studied or the heat
Destroys the thing it feeds—organic
Matter, of course, is best to raise
The famous beauty of the rose.

He smiles as if romantic lines
Could call rain down upon his plants:

    You often praised her body's grace
    And her wit, but when she left
    She cried out foolishly
    And tore off terribly gawkily . . .

And on through dinner his talk of flowers
Love and wine, until I free
Myself with the common excuse
And pass her rooms where the drawers
Are still open like stunned mouths.

The Zoo, Jackson, Mississippi, 1960

This zoo is a naked place;
Beasts of summer lodge
With habitants from ice;
Here the odd and poor

Of every kingdom come
To sample fear, where bar
And glass protect observer
And observed. The ledge

Of rocks defends their dignity
When lusts are obvious
And the dark throat bawls
For its keeper's pale meat.

Lank giraffes tread
Deliriously through heat—
At the edge of rage and sense
The eagle strains in truss.

Swimming

The eight of them were squatted along the beach
Before we even took notice. They were armed,
Or at least the man was, and we were in arm's reach.
But strange to say, we weren't just then alarmed.

Twenty of us, naked as worms, we swam
Just off the point and kept our laughing up
Until that skinny man began to ream
His piece: his first shot upstream was the slap

That caught us onto what the children wanted—
"Fun, fun, fun, fun!" they screamed. So did the wife.
We scrambled up our bank. My side chanted,
"Redneck, redneck . . ." Their man shot at our life.

Neither side was right: we should have played
The scared part, for the kids; they shouldn't
    have felt betrayed.

The Lawyer

It wasn't the Areopagus
Or even the sort of outdoor work
Some men are able to dignify—
Not what I found in the high field
The time I first checked on a murder
Witness. An old Negro was feeding
Chickens from a slot machine,
Poured grain down the top he'd pulled off
And out it came just like pure gold.
His cock and hens fought for the tray
While we got soaked by a slow March rain . . .
It wasn't the legal profession I'd sought.

He'd been known to help out before.
You went to where he was when the rest
Who'd seen the whole damn thing were deaf,
Blind, dumb and innocent as Fudgsicles.
They said once he'd kept his eyes and tongue
For twenty dollars when both sides died.
But on my day he wasn't selling.

I stood there in wet chickenshit
And shot back something about the law
And *how the hell was justice done* . . . ?
But his eyes were queer as my law was.
He wasn't rude like the new ones.
He thanked me for my offering
But said there wasn't profit in it;
So I figured he'd been talked to,
Had gotten straight just what the game was
And knew his side. I left his rooster
Winning every time, and felt
More out of place than his machine.

His Old Friend Who Sometimes Comes to Talk

In May, his last time over, he drank too much,
Was vulgar and sick by one, then wept till three—

It was all about the end of such and such
An order, but I never follow well the free
Confusion of the graceful past not memory

And I honestly suspect mortality
In general defeats him more than Lee.

The Politician's Pledge

You'd think there was heat enough all day,
With the sun the whole white sky—
But in my counties they burn things down
At night. No cool Christ in the tomb
Will do for them. They thrive on fire,
And I'll be damned if I'll feed fire.
Preachers! It's preachers I always blame.
They whine in the dusk for Zion's flames.

Make me an out-of-work mechanic
And bring my whole family down sick
If I ride one nigger again.
When it comes time for me to run
My tongue is ice—
Conditioned air in every house—
And if for that I'm not sent back,
I hope they're resurrected black.

On Hearing That the State Economic Council Believes $5000 a Year for Every White Family Will Quiet Things Down

There are pink flamingos
On metal legs in their yard
And grass is growing
Where once it was beaten hard—

There's a border of tire
Halves painted white
Where last year
Most blacks wouldn't walk at night.

Eden's Threat

Still now, at the brake's edge,
we stand, confused by the sun.

All that time! Years
it must have been, and the gunfire
along the bayous was not so bright
as this day is . . .

Years on the dead run,
the hounds near—then hidden
at night in dim pine shacks
with a lank, soft woman—

We touch our stubble faces,
the lean bones of our chins,
and we were never caught
and Eden's threat is less
where we have been.

Miracle Play

Jonathas who stabbed the Host in the ancient play
And got God's blood was fortunate, though he lost
His soul awhile.
      To think of that and the way
His doubt was healed by Christ Himself could weigh
Upon your reverie, could cause alarm
At night, when the day's hand is ripped from its arm—
When the cauldron's stew you know is you seems sin
At best . . .
      In fact, you'd hope to Hell
It *is* sin you feel . . .
      For if it's not, then the flesh you smell
Remains in the mass a common human waste,
And the god's grace to the Medieval Jew
Is the wink of history, not prophecy.

Tornadoes (for H.R.T.)

Mine wasn't as extraordinary as
My grandfather's. His came down from higher,
A classical shape, hung from the Kansas sky.
Mine stooped over the woods, a squatty cloud.
Grandfather's, like a cornucopia
Gone haywire—sucking horribly, not spilling
Plenty (unless you grant the stories it left
A bounty)—came and beat his town down flat.

Hysterical naked women were in the streets;
Fortunes like his own were thrown across
The tragical Kansas plain, his jewelry store
A blasted treasure-trove.
                              Every acre
In Kansas a sullen Populist demanding
His share—a pair of broken glasses, a diamond—
The grasses grown suddenly filthy rich,
And laughing—naked women howling all night—

His town become a waste on that rigorous land.
And he told that story each year, in still weather,
Until he died: Weeds! Diamonds gone!
And the neighbor's daughter turning around and around . . .

Mine came bucking over the trees and fell,
For a moment, to lift one dog, and that was all,
A helpless dog swung up in an awkward squall,
And nothing was beaten flat to raise a tale.

Just North of Sikeston

One night just north of Sikeston
I had a vision, or at least an insight,
Driving at fifty where before the worst
Was eyestrain. (It was within the legal limit.)

The season was spring and every truck and car
Had perfect manners, held
To their side and blinked their headlights
To keep from going blind—
A lovely thing when you think what could easily happen
On an eighteen-foot road with a lip
If people get a little out of line.
That brought the horrors, the vision,
	or what you will . . .
You see, I realized some mean to die—
Some, too much aware
Of spring and how the earth
Begins to hate them less, will fling themselves
And families across the median.
With the weather getting better, these winter men
Will cram one lane with life
To quiet the ugly wife
And free themselves and children from the long ways
I want to ride with mine for years. Dear God,
I thought, please let him kill in some other state

Tonight, as he seems to . . .
Or, better, let him die
Alone in a ploughed field,
His throat slit by his own hand—
Or in a big motel,
His pistol in his mouth—
Don't let him crush his family, or mine,
Or any other man's. Save, if you can,
A dozen lives too subtle to abide
A fury of metal. Let
No man gone out of round tear living years
On a wheel insanely rolling bloody from
The berm. It's love that dims
Our lights. It's praise that we take care to ease
Ourselves from every curve.

Notes for a Homily: The Medieval Monk Broods Over an Epic

A better ending would be for the hero to have a great illumination immediately after killing the dragon.

In that moment of light he would know that the dragon had been trying to protect him from the treasures, and that all the huffing and puffing had been because the poor beast believed that dramatics were the only thing a hero could understand.

If the hero realized this, he would have such a great sense of compunction that he would bury the dragon *and* the treasures.

He would say nothing about the fight with the dragon and he would say nothing about the treasures.

He would put an end to one curse.

Leavings

I hesitate to enter rooms
Where friends intend to be themselves;
I find myself afraid of wives
Who never mention sex until
Their husbands have gone to pee. But still
I move right in among those breasts
They say are only for baby. If

I run I'll never understand
Illogical tales, bad jokes, and men
Who horrify themselves until
They leave marks on public walls.

It's impossible to tell until
You've been. You have to go beyond
Dead Ends, on down below the sign
Into the brake, to find the wrack

Of something that lived—the hide of a cow
Caught in the vines, the hollow ribs
Of birds dried on the sand, or what
Remains of the child they say was murdered
Fifteen years ago. You have
To go in there to see if leavings
Are wastes and void of common truth.

Kalma

Kalma, "odor of the corpse," is the word
   for death with Finns, and in one myth they say
   the soul and the blood are one: they weep at graves,
   make offerings before decay. And I've heard

Finn warriors will eat the heart and the lungs
   of their dead to win the spirit back, to hold
   those best remains from the earth and the cold
   they know so well.

Yet they have no hell.

For a Neighbor Child

I yelled at you for climbing too high in our tree
   and descents like death confuse the memory
   and your falling face won't go and something more—
   the awful order of the past must be
   the necessary lie . . .

Up there at twelve you turned to kiss my son
   and now all's dark and you are younger than he.
   You had such courage, climbed the tree and fell—
   fell through limbs down thirty silent feet
   and all the age you'd learned . . .

And then you slept before you died
   and I have had to say you dreamed he'd fallen too . . .
   I could not miss your breaking skull
   and the few leaves your lover saw follow
   and you are constant in that fall . . .

A film in time continues to snap you up and down,
   a terrible reel that holds me still,
   for I praised when he wept against us great tears.

My Son's Bad Dreams

Usually he wears his mother's
    lovely manners
And carries himself as I do
    when I get my way.
He goes well with our friends, and to hear
    his regular teachers
He is wonderful
    at study and play . . .

But some nights he flounders and whines
    in a sweaty bed:
He has caught the factitious fever
    from his mother,
And from me he knows he will soon
    need more than water—
He cries out how his good days
    fill him with dread.

My Elderly Cousin (for F.S.)

In the thirties she saw three men shot down
My elderly cousin
The family's only painter,
And once in Chicago Grant Wood went for her knee.
She hardly understood
The thirties, and maybe Wood was lonely.

She paints great plains whereon there are no men
Except for her coarse father, her railing mother.
Her scapes are vicious with color—
Chartreuse Nebraska skies
Impasto vermilion stalks
No one has ever believed, and only orange hawks
For animals about that odd land sea.

I ask her to talk more of the thirties. "I'd rather
Forget the cities now," she says. Her hand
Whirls over her knee, describes her bad land.

One for the Sea

When eyes go blind or wild among the waves
The roads of water flame through corposants
And light all time remembered by the slaves
Of twenty senses from the bowels of saints,
Old zodiacs of wine and undead husks . . .

And that you say is too far gone for poetry
When of the modern tooling school. I

Have learned your way, to be exact, but fear
At times its hard lucidity, and hear
The furor of a larger, turbid time . . .

It's then I disremember style and the need
To grind verse fine, and sink my heart to the source . . .

This miraculous flailing sea recorded as culture
Is a storm of scalding salt, if I choose that course—
Or a passive beach where bodies rot, but stink not.

News Photo with a Hurricane Story

An image of a man and the wrack and the sea
  and something about to be shot forced on me
  a careful search.

At first I thought he shot
  his hat, a strange thing to do in the rain;
  then I realized the dark place was a coiled snake,
  and felt I knew why a picture like that
  was sent to state how it is when great storms break.

In awful weather, his gun's accusing line
  and the name of his town and the date
  of his natural crime
  were witnesses to fear—
  and I am sure his home washed out
  when he fell in his hate to blast that thoughtless head . . .

But I can't laugh, though through gun-crack and spatter
  he was so ignorant,
  for few should unpersonify great pain
  until the sea makes clear just what it means—
  until the wind begins to explain, to explain, to explain . . .

Overcoming Bad Weather

The wind had ripped off the roof of the R.E.A.
and the American Legion, too—there's still some justice—
or balance—or at least what's indiscriminate
continues. Rough weather all around. High water—
and of an afternoon I was leaving home
awhile to journey alone away from children
and passed the heavy cover of a sewer
that spouted two spews from its little furious holes,
geysers that were not at all baroque. High wind—

I was driving our brand new car so carefully
to balance the bottle of bourbon properly
between my legs on the floor, that it not fall down at all;
and it didn't, though I passed a flattened home
with underwear everywhere on the trees and the lawn
and passed mysterious girls, frenzied in puddles,
and compassionate politicians cleaning fish.

It sat so well erect I thought
I'd overcome bad weather and
the babble of my own dear spawn
and the romantic mounds
of water rising beneath the street . . .

I drove as if I were a galleon
and drove as if it were a kind of fun
with the fifth on the floor—and it certainly never fell
as I passed those fountains of children, and raw clouds,
and distances I'd never known
until I crashed and burned in the sun.

First Lecture

Recently I heard a friend was mad.
It seems he took to women by the score,
Went nude to teach a class of freshmen boys,
Then burned the books he loved.
No doubt this fits
Some classic case concluded and almost cured
Years ago. But I won't seek a paradox
To call him sane.
He was no Christ, and his loss
Of mind might well have led to serious crime.

He was the kind we rarely understand.
He feared the voice, was pressed to complete a clause
Without a breath—
His lungs were strong, but he weighed
Each word too carefully . . .
He knew nine languages
By heart and tried to read each line of poetry
As if it were the last the man had said.
He wanted to know what caused a hand to push pen
Or to type, he wanted to know why any man
Felt wise enough to speak
At all. This led to his fall.

Yet now they say he rests quite well,
Takes easily to therapy,
Though they have no plans to let him out,
And I hear he reads again for his board,
He reads to children and the old,
Will keep it up so long as they
Will stay and at this play all seem
To understand, for none require
The meaning of a word he reads,
And his stammering has almost stopped . . .

Which brings to mind a thought he used to say:
The end of style for honest men is clarity.

On the Lady's Clothes

Beauty is a skirt.
It's not dull clothes
Of a boy on a lady's body—
Common cloth
Wound round and separating
Lovely legs,
Not hide and hair and that
Gruff coat that hangs
To your bound knees.

Recollect the bright designs
Suggesting where
A hand with ease begins
Some transport from
The rigorous world of men,
Release again
Fantastic shapes I fear—
Make them loose and soft
And terribly easy and near.

Let me unburden you
Of this harsh array—
I've dressed you supple skins
For rare display.

Cul-de-sac

My mother lost a child while I was twelve, but it wasn't
  the way it was yesterday when my love did. My mother's
  loss had a sex and was my brother a day, for he breathed
  awhile before he died. And I cried he hadn't had a chance,
  which was true, abashed to see him dressed in blue in his
  neat box.

O he was wax, a sullen doll, and there was a preacher too
  (and a grave for his birth), saying he'd be near God's
  throne in spite of Catholics who give the cul-de-sac
  to such as he.

But it was not that way yesterday when our flesh was stooled
  or so we guess, for what I brought in the jar was after-
  birth and the cord, the doctor said.

Words for the Sexual Revolution

Such exercise over your grandfather's way
Of making love—simply because you say
He never filled your Granny's *needs*. Maybe so . . .

But it seemed the thing to do when he felt like it
Or not at all—slowly, when spring came late,
Then like a hog to fit the autumn weather.

After such, they'd sleep for hours. Don't shout.
Be patient and let them die without assault.
Let their style break down like the maiden aunt who recalled

In perfect clarity, after twenty years,
The thing she said that set it wrong and sent
Her lover sadly away. She fumbled up

To her bed, turned out the lamp and buried her head
For fifteen more. Her groans, doctors smiling,
And echoes of heavy breathing from grandfather's room

Have breached these old walls whereon you strain your hate . . .
Only a damned fool would try to muscle a dead weight.

Love Poem in Midwinter

Herein is praise for your nose
As fine as a collie's,
Praise and the famous
Silent whistle. Please

Come back in those glossy, bestial
Boots—hard legs
You've fringed with fur.
You can trust a man who begs.

For MM

I cried. It was that simple
Except for feeling like a fool
With all those tears for a blonde.
Then I felt I ought to cry more.
She lived with fear and tried

For innocence. And we mustn't
Laugh at what she dreamed—
It seems she was standing nude in church
A sacrifice for all
Her guilt and ours, which means she loved
Uncommonly. For this
And all her comedy I write—

I offer praise because
She was the way we wanted her—
Magnificent goat without stench.
And I pray the earth on her
Is gentler than our hands.

Walking Around

My dear, your buttocks shift
Diastole, systole,
They pump like a lecher's heart—

And as you move away
I praise each lady's pulse,
Each muscle of this day.

For the Lady at Her Mirror

Begin by brushing hair,
Begin the easy strokes one hundred times
And say the rime to the mirror,
And hide your hands against your eyes where lines—
A few—have taught despair.

You are a Foolishness—broken up
With vessels in the thighs
And suffering beneath the chin to pat
And pat. Your long flesh abides,
The honest bait, the ancient prop and pit . . .

Go on, Lady, fear
The fall. Fear every change of color
And pressure—but when I am near
Take growing pleasure in every cunning cover
That binds our love and common disrepair.

Domains

1

Sometimes I find it hard to concentrate
On politics
And the rugged Brotherhood of Man—
I mean to be a Populist
Who goes according to a good reformer's plan
With all the races for a swim . . .
And the local union gets my dues . . .
But still the pamphlets, tracts and speeches bring the blues
And dreams of flight
To Red and Yellow, Black and White
Who tumble on the common beach
And by wild water where
The common terror will be shared.

2

This is the way a young man has to learn . . .
Making love to economics and the faithless moon.

3

One great-great-grandfather died
At twenty-seven of rotten meat that carried worms

In the Civil War
For the Union—
But on the other side
Dr. Bourland suffered Vicksburg
Lived to write a book to state the wisdom of his life
And cried when his eyes went out.

4

I stagger with my banner everywhere
Toward a better state
But always lovely hair
Long limbs negotiate
To turn my mind from taxes
And jack the old reflexes.

5

It is all death in time I would obliterate
And rigorous confusions of the noble dead—
But be it flesh, or memory,
Or present justice in a rout,
God, give me strength to nervously admit
I am not fit
To serve at once
Two dying bodies with equal wit.